ARCTIC ALPHABET

EXPLORING THE NORTH FROM A TO Z

TEXT AND PHOTOGRAPHY BY WAYNE LYNCH

FIREFLY BOOKS

A FIREFLY BOOK

Published by Firefly Books Ltd. 1999

First Printing

Library of Congress Cataloging-in-Publication Data is available

Canadian Cataloguing in Publication Data

Lynch, Wayne
    Arctic alphabet : exploring the North from A to Z

ISBN 1-55209-336-0 (bound)
ISBN 1-55209-334-4 (pbk.)

1. Biotic communities—Arctic regions—Juvenile literature.
2. Ecology—Arctic regions—Juvenile literature. 3. English
language—Alphabet—Juvenile literature. I. Title.

QH84.1.L96   1999   j577'.0911'3   C99-930382-1

Published in Canada in 1999 by
Firefly Books Ltd.
3680 Victoria Park Avenue
Willowdale, Ontario
M2H 3K1

Published in the United States in 1999 by
Firefly Books (U.S.) Inc.
P.O. Box 1338, Ellicott Station
Buffalo, New York
14205

Produced by
Bookmakers Press Inc.
12 Pine Street
Kingston, Ontario K7K 1W1
(613) 549-4347
tcread@sympatico.ca

Design by
Janice McLean

Color separations by
Quadratone Graphics Ltd.
Toronto, Ontario

Printed and bound in Canada by
Friesens
Altona, Manitoba

Printed on acid-free paper

*The Publisher acknowledges the financial support of the
Government of Canada through the Book Publishing Industry
Development Program for its publishing activities.*

*To my loving wife Aubrey,
for all the times
she has stood by me.*

ACKNOWLEDGMENTS

Two teachers and their students deserve special
thanks for helping me with this book. Mrs. Marg
McConnell and her grade four class at Christopher
Lake School in Saskatchewan were kind enough to
review the text for me. One student, Taylor Smith,
even took the time to write a personal letter, and I
thank her for her kind words. In Calgary, Mrs. Maria
Perri and her grades five and six classes from John
W. Costello School thoroughly studied the text and
then gave me a wonderful stack of letters, poems
and drawings. Their suggestions and criticisms were
valuable and greatly appreciated.

I would also like to thank the friendly gang at
Bookmakers Press: editor Tracy Read, art director
Janice McLean and copy editor Susan Dickinson, all
of whom work quietly behind the scenes to produce
books that always make me proud.

CONTENTS

INTRODUCTION

Every year, I travel to the Arctic for a month or more to hike on the tundra and to observe and photograph the animals and birds that live there. People are surprised when I choose to visit a place where the weather can be so cold that even in the summer, it can snow on any day. There are very few hotels and restaurants in the Arctic, and I usually have only the wind and the wildlife to keep me company. Even so, my reason for returning year after year is simple: I have traveled to every continent on Earth, and the wildlife of the Arctic excites me more than any other. In the Arctic, the sky seems to stretch forever, the cool air is delicious to breathe, and the freedom of the wild animals is fascinating to watch. For me, coming back to the Arctic is like coming back to the home of an old friend.

When the ice melts in the summer in the southern Arctic, polar bears are forced to come ashore until the ocean freezes over again. Sometimes, they must wait four months or more. During this period, the bears do not eat.

Before we set out on our journey north, let me begin by explaining the three different ways people describe the Arctic. You may have already read about the Arctic Circle—an invisible line that circles the Earth's northern pole at latitude 66 degrees 32 minutes. This line marks the Arctic's southern boundary. Everything north of the Arctic Circle is part of the Arctic. In the summer in this part of

The arctic hare is the largest bunny in the world. In the Far North, arctic hares are white year-round, and they travel in large herds that may number hundreds of animals.

the world, the sun may not set for many days in a row, which is why people sometimes call the Arctic the Land of the Midnight Sun. In the small village of Grise Fiord in northern Canada, for instance, the summertime sun does not set for 77 days in a row.

Television weather people use another way to describe the Arctic. On a map, they mark all the places where the average July temperature is just 50 degrees F (10°C). They join these places together with a line and call everywhere north of this temperature line the Arctic. In North America, the line starts in northern Alaska, dips south around Hudson Bay, then curves up again to the northern tip of Labrador.

The third and most common way to describe the Arctic is with the tree line. The tree line marks the border between the northern forests and the treeless tundra. In this definition, the Arctic simply includes all the lands north of the trees. Like the 50-degree-F (10°C) temperature line, the tree line starts in northern Alaska, dips south of Hudson Bay, then swings north to northern Labrador again.

Within the Arctic, there are thousands of plants, hundreds of birds and dozens of mammals which I could write about, but that would take a book much longer than this one. Instead, I'm going to tell you about the amazing animals and plants and other phenomena that exist in the wild spaces of the North.

AURORA BOREALIS

On clear nights, the skies of the Arctic are sometimes filled with curtains and swirls of dancing light. The shapes may be colored white, green, blue or red, and they often dim and brighten, speed up and slow down as if the sky were breathing. Then, as suddenly as the lights appear, they fade, and only the stars remain in the night sky. Aurora borealis is the fancy name for these northern lights, and although the lights seem mysterious and magical, there is a simple explanation for how and why they occur.

An aurora is caused by invaders from space. The story begins on the fiery surface of the sun, where gigantic explosions occur all the time. The explosions send showers of invisible electrical sparks racing toward Earth at two million miles (3 million km) per hour. It takes two days for the sparks to reach our planet, but Earth is not easy to invade. The planet resembles a giant magnet, and the force of this magnet surrounds Earth like a blanket, protecting it from most of the electrical sparks from the sun. Even so, in the polar regions of the planet (the Arctic, as well as the Antarctic), some of the sparks manage to break through the magnetic shield. As the sparks get closer and closer to the Earth's surface, they collide with the gases in our atmosphere. These collisions, millions and millions of them, produce the light we see in the aurora.

BELUGA WHALE

In early spring, the beluga, or white, whale makes its way back to the Arctic, often when much of the ocean is still covered with thick ice. An expert at finding narrow cracks in the sea ice, the beluga uses these small areas of open water to breathe. But early spring can be a dangerous time in the Arctic, because cracks in the ice can close suddenly or freeze over. When this happens, a beluga can hold its breath for up to 20 minutes and travel almost two miles (3 km) underwater in search of a fresh patch of open water. It can also use its back to break through ice as thick as four inches (10 cm). If the ice is too thick to break, the whale can sometimes lift it enough to create an air pocket where it can take a breath and then dive again. Among whales, only the beluga and the bowhead, another whale of the Arctic, display this unusual ice-breaking behavior.

The beluga whale is different in another way: it is the only whale that scrapes off its old skin by rubbing on the rough gravel bottom of shallow rivers. Scientists believe that the warmer, less salty water of the arctic rivers helps to loosen the whale's outer layer of skin, making it easier for the animal to rub itself clean. More than 1,700 belugas have been counted at one time congregating in a single river.

CARIBOU

The caribou lives farther north than does any other member of the deer family, and it has developed a number of ways to survive in its chilly homeland.

The caribou has small ears for its size and a short, blunt nose, and both its ears and nose are completely covered with hair. Tuktu, the Inuit name for the caribou, also has shorter legs than do other members of the deer family that live in warmer, more southern climates, such as elk or moose. As a further protection from the cold, the caribou has a warm, deep coat, whose hairs are hollow and kinky. This design allows the hairs to trap a layer of warm air close to the animal's skin and thus insulate it from the cold. The hollow hairs also make it easier for a caribou to float in the water. It is a good swimmer and can easily cross large rivers and lakes.

Another caribou response to the cold arctic winters is to migrate to the forests farther south. Some caribou may walk for many weeks to reach the trees. On the edge of the forest, the snow is less packed by the wind, so it is easier for the caribou to reach the plants it feeds on in winter. The name caribou comes from a Micmac native word meaning "shoveler," because the animal uses its broad hooves to dig through the snow in winter to uncover food.

DUCKS & GEESE

In North America, roughly 15 kinds of ducks and six or seven kinds of geese spend the summer in the Arctic. Although ducks and geese look similar to each other, they are surprisingly different in many ways. Most geese are larger than ducks, and generally, male and female geese look alike. Male and female ducks, on the other hand, often look completely different. Usually, female ducks have plain brown feathers, while the males sport brightly colored plumage.

Nor do geese and ducks share the same diet. Geese eat mainly plants, while ducks eat not only plants but also fish, crustaceans and aquatic insects.

Another way in which ducks and geese are very distinct is in how they raise a family. Most ducks, except some of the eider ducks, mate with a new partner every summer, and the male and female break up soon after the eggs are laid. The male duck never helps to raise the ducklings. Goose partners, on the other hand, may remain together for their entire lives, and the male goose always helps to raise the goslings. During the nesting season, the male goose defends the nest from trespassers, shares in warming the eggs and, after they have hatched, protects the goslings from predators. The pair stays together even when the birds migrate south in autumn.

EAGLE

With its butcher beak, 2½-inch-long (6 cm) curved talons and 6-foot (2 m) wingspan, the golden eagle is the largest bird of prey in the Arctic. It is also a powerful hunter. The eagle glides out of the sky to catch fat hoary marmots, arctic hares, ground squirrels and fast-flying ptarmigan. A hungry eagle will also clean up the carcass scraps of a muskox killed by wolves or scavenge geese that have died from exhaustion after their long spring migration.

An interesting feeding habit is displayed by the golden eagle when it teams up with a grizzly bear. One June, a pair of grizzlies in the Canadian Arctic killed five muskox calves in a single day. The bears ate only two of the animals, and the next day, a golden eagle claimed one of the remaining carcasses. Eagles often keep track of grizzlies, even when they are hunting much smaller prey. In Alaska, a scientist watched a golden eagle follow a grizzly for an hour and a half as the bear dug up the tundra trying to catch ground squirrels in their burrows. Each time the bear moved on, the eagle followed and perched on the ground nearby. Such patience pays off. While the grizzly was busy digging up the squirrel's front door, the eagle was sometimes able to catch a ground squirrel trying to escape through a rear tunnel.

FOX

Found in all the lands surrounding the Arctic Ocean, the arctic fox is the most northern fox in the world. Although it weighs no more than a house cat, this small fox is a great wanderer—its tracks have even been found far out on the sea ice very close to the North Pole.

The arctic fox is a predator that always seems to be on the move. On land, it sniffs out bird eggs and chases seabirds on the narrow ledges of dangerous cliffs. On snow, it listens for the rustlings of lemmings and voles in their tunnels below and pounces on nestlings hiding on the tundra. On the sea ice, the fox follows polar bears, stealing scraps from the mighty hunters, and digs out baby ringed seals hiding in snow caves. When an arctic fox has eaten all it can hold, it may continue to hunt, hiding the extra food in a crevice in some rocks, under a willow bush or in a hole dug on the tundra. The fox has a good memory, and when hunting is poor, it returns to these caches and sniffs out the stored food, even when it is buried beneath 28 inches (70 cm) of snow. An arctic fox in Greenland really stocked up for a hungry day: in one spot, it stored 38 seabirds, four snow buntings (a sparrow-sized bird) and a large pile of eggs.

GLACIER

There are thousands of glaciers in the Arctic, and they come in all sizes. Some are small patches of ice just a few hundred feet wide. Others are rivers of ice that flow for 100 miles (160 km) or more. Some glaciers are so large that they could almost bury an entire country. That is the case in Greenland, where glaciers cover the entire landscape except for a narrow strip around the coast.

It takes thousands of years for a glacier to form, but it happens in a very simple way. If all the snow from the previous winter has not melted by the end of summer, it is buried by new snow the following winter. When this happens summer after summer, the old snow gets deeper and deeper. Eventually, because of the weight of the snow piled on top of it, the deepest snow turns into ice. As time goes on, the ice gets thicker. Finally, it begins to move, and a glacier is born. Most glaciers flow so slowly that they don't seem to be moving at all, but some of them can move several inches or even a few feet in a single day. The fastest-moving glacier in the Arctic is in Greenland. If you were to have a picnic in front of that glacier, you might have to move before you finished eating. The glacier can advance over two feet (60 cm) in one hour!

HIBERNATION

Some of the small animals of the Arctic curl up and sleep through the winter. This is called hibernation. If you could shrink yourself to the size of a chipmunk and crawl into the burrow of a hibernating arctic ground squirrel, this is what you would find: The squirrel would be curled into a tight ball, with its tail wrapped around its head. Its nose would be cold and its body almost frozen. The squirrel would be in such a deep sleep that if you poked it with your finger, nothing would happen. You could even roll it on the ground like a bowling ball, and it still might not wake up.

A hibernating ground squirrel sleeps quietly like this throughout most of the winter, but every two weeks or so, it suddenly begins to shiver. The shivering warms up the squirrel's body, and within a few hours, it is awake again. The dozy squirrel then relieves itself, stretches a few times and, believe it or not, immediately goes back to sleep again for another two weeks. The ground squirrel is a sleepyhead not because it is lazy but because this is the only way it can survive in winter. By hibernating and staying cool and asleep, the small squirrel burns the fat on its body very slowly. It is therefore able to remain underground for many months, awaiting the return of warm weather.

INUIT

When I was a boy, almost everyone called the people who lived in the Arctic "Eskimos." The word means "eater of raw flesh," and white people intended it as an insult. The first white people who traveled to the Arctic thought that Eskimos were wild and savage and not as good as white people. They soon learned they were wrong.

Eskimos had lived in the cold, difficult land of the Arctic for thousands of years. They had learned how to hunt seals, whales and caribou with harpoons and bows and arrows. They knew how to travel by dogsled and kayak. They could build a tent out of animal skins and bones or an igloo from blocks of snow. And they could make clothing as warm as anything available today. The Eskimos were not wild. They were smart people who lived where no white person was able to live.

Today, many North American Eskimos prefer to be called Inuit rather than Eskimos. In their language, the word Inuit means "the people." Some Inuit continue to hunt and fish as their ancestors did, but many have regular jobs. There are Inuit teachers, doctors, nurses and music stars. The Inuit are proud of their history, and they are an essential part of the Arctic.

JAEGER

In the world of birds, stealing food from other birds is uncommon, but in the Arctic, there is a bird family that excels at it—the jaeger (pronounced YAY-ger) family. Although these feathered pirates are close relatives of gulls, they behave more like eagles. Jaegers have hooked beaks and sharp, curved claws on their webbed feet. They are also strong flyers able to turn in the air quickly and climb and dive like fighter jets. Hunting jaegers steal food from any bird they can bully around, but they attack seabirds most often, especially terns, gulls and puffins.

First, the jaegar searches for a seabird that is returning from the ocean with a beak or belly full of fish. Once the jaeger has a target, it swoops down from above or makes a head-on attack that forces the seabird to slow down. As the seabird puts on its brakes, the jaeger may snatch the food right out of its mouth. More often, though, the seabird swerves out of the way, and the chase is on. The jaeger follows the seabird closely, sometimes tugging at its wingtips and tail trying to throw it off balance. The jaeger doesn't always win, but when it does, the frightened seabird spits out the fish it is carrying. The sharp-eyed pirate then swerves immediately, often catching the stolen fish in midair.

K

KITTIWAKE

The kittiwake is a pretty gray-and-white arctic gull that owes its unusual name to the sound it makes when it calls. Thousands of these gulls have been known to nest together on one cliff, and you can imagine the noise when so many birds are screaming "kittiwake, kittiwake, kittiwake" as loudly as they can.

The kittiwake is not like other gulls you may have seen along the ocean coast or in a parking lot eating stale french fries from the garbage cans beside a fast-food restaurant. Most gulls lay their eggs on the ground. Soon after they hatch, the chicks run away from home, hiding in the grass and returning only at mealtimes. But kittiwakes nest on a high, steep cliff. Because it is such a dangerous place to live, kittiwake chicks don't run away from home after they hatch. They sit quietly in the nest like fuzzy little couch potatoes.

Kittiwake parents are unable to recognize their own chicks, so they will give food to any chick they find in their nest. Biologists have occasionally played tricks on kittiwake parents to prove this. In one case, a biologist put a large cormorant chick in a kittiwake nest. A cormorant chick is black, with a long beak and a neck like a snake. It looks very different from a kittiwake chick. Nevertheless, the kittiwake parents did not seem to notice the intruder and fed the new chick as if it were one of the family.

LOUSEWORT

Most people think of the Arctic as a frozen land covered by ice and snow year-round, but that's not all the Arctic can be. It can be warm in summer, when the snow sometimes disappears for two months or more and the ground is covered with flowers of many different colors. One of my favorite arctic flowers is the lousewort. Inuit children suck on lousewort flowers for the sweet nectar inside. They call the flowers bumblebee flowers, because they attract big orange-and-black bumblebees that also like the sweet nectar inside the blossoms. It's hard to forget the name of these flowers because it is so strange, and the story of how they got this name is just as strange.

Long ago in England and Scotland, lousewort flowers grew in the fields where poor farmers kept their cows and sheep. The fields did not have much grass for the animals to eat, and the animals were often thin and unhealthy and had bloodsucking lice living on them. The farmers did not understand that because they were in poor health, the cattle and sheep had lice. Instead, they believed the lice came from the flowers that grew in the fields, so they named the flower lousewort, which means lice plant. Many years later, when the first English explorers came to the Arctic, they gave these flowers the same name as those which grew in the fields back home.

MOSQUITO

The Arctic is famous for its mosquitoes—pesky insects that drill for blood on every patch of unprotected skin they can find. Only the female mosquitoes are vampires; the blood they drink helps them produce more eggs. Male mosquitoes drink plant nectar, and they never bother people. Humans can protect themselves from female mosquitoes by wearing heavy clothes, gooey insect repellent and funny head nets, but what happens to wild animals when the she-devil mosquitoes go looking for blood?

During mosquito season in the Arctic, muskoxen search out the last patches of unmelted snow to use as resting places. The cold snow keeps most of the mosquitoes away. Even the mighty polar bear has been known to dig deep underground tunnels, the same way the marmot (pictured above) does, where it can snooze and not be bugged. Sometimes, hungry mosquitoes have even crawled inside a cracked snow goose egg to feed on the gosling before it has hatched.

But the animal that suffers the most is the caribou. During the arctic summer, great clouds of the insects can suddenly appear overnight. When this happens, the caribou join in large herds and head toward the shore of the ocean, where the winds are stronger and therefore keep some of the insects away. When the wind dies down, the caribou are often bitten so viciously that they buck and stampede, running until they are exhausted. Only when cold weather returns to the Arctic do the mosquitoes finally disappear.

NARWHAL

Long ago, in the time of castles and dungeons, the most popular way to kill an enemy was with poison. And it was commonly believed that the only way to protect yourself against being poisoned was with the horn of a magical animal called the unicorn. If you dipped a piece of the unicorn's horn into your food and the food bubbled or foamed, it was probably a good idea to skip lunch.

The unicorn looked like a horse but had a long spiral horn growing from its forehead. Of course, the unicorn was a fairy-tale animal. The ivory horn, however, was based on something very real—it came from the head of an arctic whale, the narwhal. The wily Vikings hunted narwhals in the Arctic and kept the source of these horns a secret. The narwhal's horn, which can grow half as long as its body, does not really detect poison in food. But people thought it could and were willing to pay large amounts of gold to buy the horn.

The narwhal is a small whale with a blubbery gray body that stretches the length of a large car. Only male narwhals have the famous spiral ivory horn, which is not a horn at all but an overgrown tooth, or tusk, that grows out of the left side of its upper jaw. With no other teeth besides its tusk, the narwhal catches fish and other food and either gums it to death or swallows it alive.

Photograph © Glenn Williams

OWL

The beautiful white snowy owl is one of the largest and most powerful owls in the world, and it lives farther north than any other owl. It has bright white feathers year-round. When the female snowy owl lays her eggs in summer, the tundra is often brown and green, making it easy for hungry predators to spot the white owl.

Like many owls, the female snowy owl is larger than the male, but the male is often more fierce. The male may attack any animal that comes too close to its nest, and the bird fights with dangerous weapons: its hooked beak has a razor-sharp edge, its feet are large and powerful, and its toes are armed with sharp curved talons.

Arctic foxes are easily driven off by an angry snowy owl, and even large arctic wolves run when an owl begins to dive-bomb them. The snowy owl usually makes a surprise attack from the rear, and if it extends its talons, it can cut its enemies deeply as it swoops by. The brave male may even attack humans, who are many times larger than it is. Arctic biologists have often been attacked by fierce snowy owls and have sometimes required stitches to repair the deep wounds.

POLAR BEAR

Most animals that live in the Arctic give birth to their young in spring, with the return of warm temperatures. Female polar bears are different. They have their cubs during the cold, dark months of winter.

At birth, a polar bear cub is barely bigger than a squirrel. It is toothless, its eyes are closed, and the short fine body hair makes it look almost naked. The cub is not much to look at, but it sure can scream, which it does whenever it is hungry, cold or frightened.

When a polar bear cub is born, the mother is buried inside the shelter of a snow cave and has not been able to eat for many months. A newborn cub is far too small to travel, and besides, it could never survive the cold weather of winter. As a result, the mother bear must wait while her cubs grow larger, and they need to grow as quickly as possible. A mother polar bear's rich milk is thicker than whipping cream and contains lots of energy. After several months of nursing, the young polar bear cubs are as big as a medium-sized dog. Soon afterward, the hungry mother leads her cubs out of the family den onto the ice, where they will slowly learn to become the great white hunters of the Arctic.

QIVIUT

The muskox is the most common large land animal in many places in the Arctic. Inuit call the big, shaggy mammal oomingmak, which means the bearded one. To survive the strong winds, blizzards and freezing cold of an Arctic winter, the muskox needs a thick, warm coat. This animal actually has two coats in one. On the outside is a heavy coat of guard hairs. Some of the guard hairs are over two feet (60 cm) long and hang around the animal's legs like a grass skirt. Underneath the guard hairs is a dense coat of soft, fine wool, which the muskox sheds every summer. For a month or so, the animal has great tattered clumps of messy wool hanging from its body. Eventually, the wool gets caught on bushes or blows loose in the wind. Afterward, small birds may gather bits of what the Inuit call qiviut (pronounced KIV-ee-ute) to line their nests.

Much softer than sheep's wool, qiviut is also many times warmer. Because of this, Inuit sometimes gather qiviut from the tundra and use it to knit clothing. Qiviut makes such soft, warm clothing that some people in Alaska keep up to 100 muskoxen on a farm so that they can collect the wool more easily.

RAVEN

Although humans think a clever insult is to call someone a birdbrain, many birds are smarter than you might think. One of the brainiest of all birds is the common raven.

There are a number of ways you can tell that the raven is no ordinary birdbrain. To begin with, it's a chatterbox. A raven uses at least 30 different calls. It is very good at imitating other animals as well, including humans. The raven also has a good memory. Like the arctic fox, it stores extra food for another day. In one case, a hunting raven hid over a thousand seabird eggs, burying each one separately in a different spot on the tundra. Later, the bird found and ate every one of the eggs, an amazing example of its memory.

Smart animals are usually playful animals, and among birds, the raven plays more than most. In the air, a raven may fly upside down for a moment or two, chase another raven in a game of tag or do acrobatic rolls like pilots at an air show. The raven also plays on the ground. One raven was spotted sliding headfirst down a snowbank on its back, with its feet sticking up in the air. The raven slid down the snowbank four times before it flew away. So whenever you hear someone described as a birdbrain, think about the raven, one of the smartest birds in the world.

SEALS

All the seals in the Arctic are expert divers, and all of them can hold their breath underwater for 20 minutes or more. Most humans cannot hold their breath for even one minute. Try to hold your breath for as long as you can. What happens inside your body when you stop breathing? Your temperature stays the same, your heart keeps beating, and your blood continues to move around as usual. But one important thing does change as you hold your breath. The oxygen in your blood slowly burns away, and if the oxygen gets too low, you will faint.

When scuba divers go underwater, they carry extra oxygen with them inside tanks strapped to their backs. A seal also carries extra oxygen, but in a very different way than a scuba diver. A seal has almost twice as much blood in its body as a human does, so it can carry more oxygen. A seal also stores oxygen in its muscles.

Two other things happen inside a seal's body that do not happen inside ours when we hold our breath. When a seal dives, its heart slows down and blood flows only to the animal's heart and brain; very little circulates to the rest of its body. In this way, the seal saves the oxygen in its blood for the two most important parts of its body: the main engine (the heart) and the central computer (the brain). This allows it to stay underwater for a long time.

TERN

When it comes to long-distance flying, no bird does it better than the arctic tern. At the end of each summer, after the nesting season, the tern leaves the Arctic and flies south, very far south—all the way to Antarctica, at the other end of the Earth. When it arrives, it is the southern summer, and the tern spends the next four months fishing among the icebergs of Antarctica. Then, as winter returns to Antarctica, the tern flies all the way back to the Arctic, just in time for the northern summer.

In a single year, an arctic tern may fly 30,000 miles (50,000 km), farther than any other animal migration on Earth. It's hard to imagine how far that is, so let's think of it in another way. An arctic tern can live for more than 20 years. In its lifetime, this small bird will fly the same distance between the Arctic and the Antarctic as it would if it were to fly to the moon and back.

The arctic tern is not only a very strong flyer but also a very good navigator. Each summer, after flying halfway around the world, many arctic terns return to the same small piece of arctic tundra where they nested the year before. One remarkable tern from Greenland came back to the same nest 19 years in a row.

UNDER THE ICE

In the middle of winter in the northern parts of the Arctic, the sun may disappear for months at a time. At the North Pole, for example, the sun does not rise for half the year. Naturally, it is a big event when light finally returns to the dark land. As the days grow longer, the weak sunlight allows tiny plants to grow on the underside of the sea ice, like an upside-down garden. These plants, called algae, usually form a thick green and brown scum on the underside of the ice and sometimes hang in long waving strands.

Many small sea animals graze on the algae, like cows in a field of grass. Amphipods, or sea lice, are one group of algae-eaters. Sea lice look like shrimp that have been flattened on the sides, and hundreds of them can live under one small piece of ice. Although sea lice eat plants, they also hunt and eat each other, and like piranhas, they will follow the scent of blood and swarm over a dead or dying animal. Within days, nothing but bones remain. Scientists occasionally use sea lice to help them with their work. When researchers find a dead animal whose bones they want to keep, they hang the carcass in the water, and sea lice chew off all the fat and meat, leaving a nice clean skeleton.

VOLES & LEMMINGS

Voles and lemmings are tough little animals that travel under the snow throughout the winter. Unlike marmots and ground squirrels, which hibernate, voles and lemmings do not sleep away the winter. To stay active, these small animals must protect themselves from the cold. At the beginning of winter, voles and lemmings move to areas where the snowdrifts are deepest. Here, they dig tunnels that connect their winter nests to different feeding areas hidden beneath the snow. Deep snow protects them from the strong winter winds and very cold temperatures. Inside the snow tunnels, the temperature is cool, often very near the freezing point, but it is still much warmer than it would be without the protective blanket of snow.

Voles and lemmings have the perfect body shape to keep them warm in their winter tunnels—they are shaped like a ball. Nothing sticks out from their fat, rounded bodies. Their legs are short, their small ears are hidden in long fur, and they have hardly any tails at all. Lemmings even have fur on the soles of their feet to keep them warm.

As we have seen, arctic mammals survive the winter in different ways. Some, like caribou and beluga whales, migrate and move south, where conditions are easier; others, like marmots and ground squirrels, hibernate; and some, like voles and lemmings, hide beneath the snow—three different solutions to the same problem.

WALRUS

Its large ivory tusks make the walrus easy to recognize. A pair of tusks can be up to 30 inches (75 cm) long, about the length of a child's baseball bat.

A walrus uses its tusks for a number of different jobs. The tusks make a good sledgehammer to chop holes in the ice in winter, or they can be used as a weapon against predators, such as killer whales, polar bears and humans. A walrus may also use its tusks to pull itself out of the water onto a floating piece of ice. This explains the walrus's scientific name, *Odobenus*, which means "tooth walker."

During the winter mating season, adult male walruses use their tusks to jab each other as they fight to win a female. As extra protection, the skin on a walrus's neck and shoulders is almost two inches (5 cm) thick and is covered with knobs that help to prevent serious injuries.

For a long time, many people believed that the walrus used its tusks mainly as a rake to find crabs, clams and worms on the ocean floor. The truth is, the walrus never uses its tusks to find food. Instead, it closes its eyes and feels for food in the mud on the bottom of the ocean with its thick whiskers. When it finds something tasty, it slurps it up.

XANTHORIA

Lichens (pronounced LIKE-ens) are the most common group of plants that grow in the Arctic. Many lichens don't look like plants at all. They look more like blobs of black, yellow and orange paint splattered on rocks, old bones and antlers. Lichens are probably the toughest plants in the world. There is no place too cold, too windy or too dark for lichens to grow. Because lichens are so tough, it is not surprising that these plants can live for a very long time. Some arctic lichens are thousands of years old—they began to grow before Christopher Columbus landed in North America!

One of the most colorful arctic lichens is the jewel lichen. It is a crusty bright orange lichen that grows in many places in the Arctic. Scientists call the jewel lichen xanthoria (pronounced zan-THOR-ee-ah), which is a real tongue twister of a name. Believe it or not, the jewel lichen grows best in places where wild animals and birds relieve themselves. Large birds such as eagles, hawks and falcons often perch on the same rocks day after day to hunt and to watch for trespassers. While they are waiting, the big birds squirt out blasts of whitewash that splash over the rocks. The whitewash encourages the jewel lichen's growth, and the rocks become painted with the orange plants. To locate these nests from an airplane, scientists look for rocks where this colorful lichen grows.

YELLOWCOAT

Many seal pups in the Arctic are born on the surface of the sea ice in early spring. It is a cold, windy nursery, and the pups can easily be found by wild hunters, such as arctic foxes and polar bears. To protect the pups, female seals often give birth in areas of sea ice that crack and break into pieces. Polar bears and foxes don't want to fall into the frigid water, so they generally avoid this kind of ice.

Because the ice can break at any moment, newborn seal pups may be tossed into the icy water before they are big enough to swim. As a result, a seal pup must grow very quickly and add a thick protective layer of blubber to its body.

The newborn harp seal pup, called a yellowcoat because of its straw-colored fur, grows so quickly that after just 12 days, its mother goes off on her own, leaving the pup to fend for itself. At birth, a harp seal pup weighs around 22 pounds (10 kg), the size of a small dog. The baby seal is skinny, and its head looks too big for its body. After less than two weeks, the pup weighs almost 75 pounds (35 kg). Now it looks like a stuffed sausage with a black nose and whiskers stuck on one end. Amazingly, the yellowcoat gains four pounds (2 kg) every day.

ZOOPLANKTON

Microscopic animals drift around the oceans of the Arctic. They are so small that you will probably never see them. They are called zooplankton, and most people don't even know that they are in the water. There are thousands of different kinds of zooplankton, and although it is invisible, zooplankton is one of the most important parts of the Arctic food chain. Without it, there would be no walruses or seals, no beluga whales or narwhals and no seabirds or polar bears.

The Arctic food chain begins with tiny drifting plants called plant plankton. The plant plankton is eaten by many different kinds of small zooplankton. Large zooplankton then hunt and eat the small zooplankton. Afterwards, small fish gobble up the large zooplankton, and seals gulp down the fish. The seals then haul themselves out onto the ice to rest, and they get caught by polar bears.

So, as you can see, to build a polar bear, you must start with zooplankton and work your way up.

MEET THE AUTHOR

Dr. Wayne Lynch has been a wildlife photographer and nature writer for most of his adult life. In the past 20 years, he has traveled to every continent on Earth to observe and study wild animals in different wilderness areas. In 1998, he photographed giant anteaters and anacondas in the grasslands of Brazil, the wildebeest migration in East Africa, rare yellow-eyed penguins in New Zealand and colorful ducks on the Canadian prairies. Although he visits exotic locations all over the world, his favorite place is still the Arctic, and in 1999, he will spend two months camping and hiking on Baffin Island in the High Arctic of Canada.

Dr. Wayne Lynch, seen here with one of his northern pals, a great gray owl.

But Dr. Lynch believes that the beauty and excitement of nature is all around us, and you don't have to visit faraway lands to see and enjoy wild creatures. There are wild creatures in the fields and parks right in the center of our major cities. All you need to appreciate them is a curious mind.

Photograph © Dr. Gordon Court